DISCOVERING
RUSSIA

By Penelope Perrin

A ZOË BOOK

A ZOË BOOK

© 1994 Zoë Books Limited

Devised and produced by
Zoë Books Limited
15 Worthy Lane
Winchester
Hampshire SO23 7AB
England

First published in Great Britain in 1994 by
Zoë Books Limited
15 Worthy Lane
Winchester
Hampshire SO23 7AB

A record of the CIP data is available from the British Library.

ISBN 1 874488 23 1

Printed in Italy by Grafedit SpA
Research: Deborah Tyler
Design: Jan Sterling, Sterling Associates
Picture research: Victoria Sturgess
Map: Gecko Limited
Production: Grahame Griffiths

Photographic acknowledgments
The publishers wish to acknowledge, with thanks, the following photographic sources:

Cover: Robert Harding Picture Library; title page: Tony Stone Images; 5 The Hutchison Library / Vladimir Bireus; 6 Tony Stone Images; 7l & r Robert Harding Picture Library; 8 Bruce Coleman Ltd / Hans Reinhard; 9l Robert Harding Picture Library; 9r, 10 Zefa; 11l Bruce Coleman Ltd / Steve Kaufman; 11r, 12 Magnum Photos/Fred Mayer; 13l The Hutchison Library / Victoria Juleva; 13r Impact Photos / Bradshaw; 14 Zefa; 15l Magnum Photos/Peter Marlow; 15r Robert Harding Picture Library; 16 Zefa; 17l Robert Harding Picture Library; 17r Zefa; 18 The Hutchison Library / Igor Gavrilov; 19l Zefa; 19r The Hutchison Library / Victoria Juleva; 20 Robert Harding Picture Library; 21l Magnum Photos / Abbas; 21r The Hutchison Library / John Egan; 22 Sporting Pictures; 23l The Wernher Collection, Luton Hoo; 23r Zefa; 24 Robert Harding Picture Library; 25 The Kobal Collection; 26, 27l & r Mary Evans Picture Library; 28 Mary Evans / Alexander Meledin Collection; 29l Peter Newark's Military Pictures; 29r DDA Photo Library

Cover: *St Basil's Cathedral, Moscow*

Title page: *A boy fishing at St Petersburg*

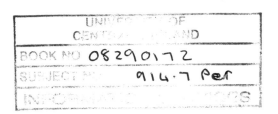

Contents

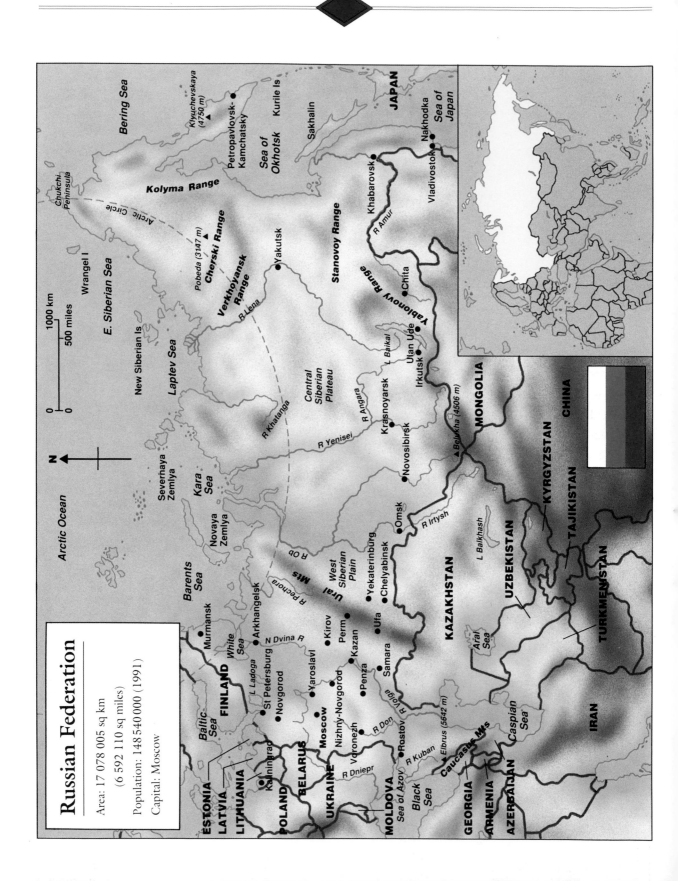

Russian Federation

Area: 17 078 005 sq km
(6 592 110 sq miles)

Population: 148 540 000 (1991)

Capital: Moscow

Privetstviye!

That is how the Russians say 'welcome!'. When they write the word down, it looks like this: Приветствие . The Russian language has an alphabet of 31 letters and two special signs. The script was first written down by a Greek Christian, St Cyril, and so it is called Cyrillic. The alphabet is over 1100 years old.

Russian belongs to the Slav group of languages, which includes Polish and Czech. It is spoken by at least 25 million Russians who live abroad as well as in Russia itself.

Over 147 million people live in Russia, but they are not all Russians. The country is also home to Tartars, Cossacks, Bashkirs and many other peoples. Some of these are Russian-speakers, others have their own languages and traditions.

The name 'Russia' should really be used to describe the land between the White Sea and the Caucasus Mountains, in the eastern part of Europe. The country's proper name is the 'Russian Federation'. It extends far beyond the Ural Mountains, across Asia to Siberia and the Far East. However, many people refer to the whole of this region as Russia.

It is hard to imagine the vast area of the Russian Federation. It is 70 times the size of Britain, and nearly twice the size of the United States. It covers 11 of the world's time zones. As the sun sets in western Russia, it is already rising in the Far East!

Changing borders

In 1922, after three years of fighting, Russia joined itself to nearby lands to form the world's biggest country, the Soviet Union. Seventy years later the Union came to an end. It broke up into separate countries once again.

Eleven of these kept up their old links by forming a group called the Commonwealth of Independent States (CIS). Russia is the biggest CIS member by far. It is still the largest country in the world.

Visitors from beyond the Urals look around Moscow's Red Square.

West of the Urals

The beautiful city of St Petersburg is built on over 100 islands at the mouth of the River Neva, on the Gulf of Finland. From here ships can sail to Baltic and North Sea ports.

St Petersburg is home to five million people. It was the capital city of Russia between 1713 and 1918, and has many fine buildings, as well as statues, bridges, canals and fountains. The Winter Palace and the Hermitage house some of the world's greatest art collections. St Petersburg lies so far north that in the summer the sky stays light all through the night. Some short stories written by the great Russian writer, Fyodor Dostoevsky (1821-81), describe these 'White Nights'.

Russia has another western port called Kaliningrad. Once this was a German city called Königsberg, and many Germans from other parts of the old Soviet Union were later re-settled here. Today it is a base for the Russian navy and a centre of trade. Since the break-up of the Soviet Union it has been cut off from the rest of the Russian Federation by the countries of Poland and Lithuania.

St Petersburg from the River Neva

What's in a name?

Many Russian cities and streets have changed their names over the years. The name St Petersburg dates back to 1703. In 1914 the city became known as Petrograd (the Russian words for 'Peter' and 'city') and, in 1924, it became Leningrad. That was in honour of Vladimir Ilyich Lenin, a communist revolutionary who became the first leader of the Soviet Union.

The communists were opposed to the private ownership of land and business. The Communist Party was in power until 1991 – and then Leningrad once again became St Petersburg. Taxi-drivers threatened to go on strike if any more street names were changed!

Cities of the west

Most Russians live in the European part of the federation, where there are many large industrial cities. Both Nizhny-Novgorod, known as Gorky during the communist period, and Samara (formerly Kuybyshev) produce locomotives, aircraft and vehicles. Rostov, on the River Don, has shipbuilding yards, textile mills and chemical factories.

The snowy peak of Elbrus towers above the Caucasus range of mountains.

The Volga is Europe's longest river.

European Russia

The whole of western Europe would fit into the great plain that lies to the west of the Ural Mountains. This is a land of pine and birch forests, bitterly cold in winter and warm and dry in summer. Most of the region is only about 200 metres (656 ft) above sea level.

The plain is drained by great rivers. The Volga is Europe's longest, flowing 3690 kilometres (2293 miles) from its source, northwest of Moscow, to the Caspian Sea. There are other natural wonders, too. Ladoga, near St Petersburg, is the biggest lake in Europe. Far to the south, the Caspian is the largest inland sea in the world.

Elbrus, in the Caucasus Mountains, is Europe's highest peak at 5642 metres (18 511 ft). The Caucasus Mountains rise from rolling farmland to form the Russian Federation's southern border, with Georgia. The Ural Mountains are lower, tree-covered hills which form Europe's border with Asia.

Into Siberia

From Moscow, the Russian capital, you can catch a train eastwards to the Sea of Japan. The journey takes over a week! On the way, the train passes a stone column which marks the border between Europe and Asia. Ahead lies Siberia.

The West Siberian Plain is a vast area of flat land, with marshes and great river systems, such as the Ob and the Irtysh. The plain stretches from the frozen lands of the Arctic in the north to the grassy steppes and hot sandy deserts of Kazakhstan in the south. In between lie endless forests, known as the *taiga*.

Between the Yenisei and the Lena rivers the land rises to form the Central Siberian Plateau.

Siberia means 'the sleeping land'. There are only two seasons. Winter is long and bitter, with snow from September to May. The temperature can drop to minus 60°C (minus 76°F). Summer is short but very warm. Then the temperatures rise to about 30°C (86°F) and wildflowers and berries grow quickly. This is the land of the wolf and the brown bear, which is Russia's national symbol.

The brown bear is a symbol of Russia. Here, two young ones tussle in the snow.

A Trans-Siberian locomotive nears Barabinsk.

The world's longest track

The Trans-Siberian Railway runs for 9438 kilometres (5865 miles) from Moscow to Nakhodka on the Sea of Japan. It was built in 1905 and became one of the most famous railways in the world. Today it stops at 90 stations and takes 8 days 4 hours and 25 minutes precisely! Modern international branch lines run south to Mongolia and China.

At the centre of Russia

The Trans-Siberian Railway passes many villages made up of small wooden houses with carved shutters and fenced yards.

This railway also links towns and large cities, where large blocks of flats are surrounded by smoking factory chimneys. Siberia's largest cities are mostly in the south, near Russia's border with Kazakhstan. Omsk and Novosibirsk both have populations of over a million. Much of Siberia is an empty wilderness, but it has untold wealth in the form of natural resources. Western Siberia supplied half of the oil produced for the old Soviet Union. It has natural gas and

valuable minerals including iron ore, diamonds and gold. The Trans-Siberian railway carries huge amounts of timber from the region's forests.

People say that God dropped a sack of treasures on Siberia. He was so cross at losing them that he cursed the region with permanently frozen soil, forest bugs and midges!

The 'Pearl of Siberia'

This 'pearl' is really a beautiful lake, near the town of Irkutsk. Baikal is the deepest lake in the world, plunging to 1940 metres (6365 feet) and containing more fresh water than any other. Only one river, the Angara, flows out of Baikal, but 336 rivers flow in! Over 50 kinds of fish live in the lake. In the winter, the local Buryat people walk out from the shore to fish through holes in the ice.

The beautiful shores of Lake Baikal

Arctic Russia

МЕХАНИК ЖЕЛТОВСКИЙ
ВЛАДИВОСТОК

Stranded in a northern port until spring

Northern Russia is a land set in ice. The long coastline of European Russia and of Siberia borders the Arctic Ocean. Shipping can reach the western port of Murmansk, but Arkhangelsk is only kept open through the year by icebreakers. Both of these cities have around half a million inhabitants.

Beyond the White Sea, there are lonely headlands and islands – home to polar bears, seals and the rare Laptev walrus. Novaya Zemlya, Svernaya Zemlya and

Reindeer herds feed on mosses and lichens.

the New Siberian Islands point towards the North Pole, where the frozen ocean never melts.

Cape Chelyuskin, on the Taymyr peninsula, is the northernmost point of the Russian mainland. It lies about 1500 kilometres (930 miles) north of the Arctic Circle.

Across the tundra

The open landscape of Arctic Russia is covered by snow for most of the year. Even when the snow melts, the soil remains deep-frozen below two metres (six feet). No trees can grow here, but there are mosses and lichens and small shrubs. This kind of land is called tundra.

In the south this landscape gives way to the forests and swamps of the *taiga*. A quarter of all the world's forests are to be found within the borders of the Russian Federation.

On rivers such as the Lena, the winter ice is so thick that it is used as a road by trucks and cars. In summer, barges can travel along the same waterway.

Herders and hunters

The few people who live in Arctic Russia survive by herding reindeer, wildfowling, hunting and fishing. A few of them follow the traditional way of life, wandering with their herds, eating reindeer meat and wearing clothes of deerskin or fur. However most of them have now settled down in villages. They wear modern anoraks and hunt with rifles.

Peoples of the Arctic include the Lapps, on Russia's border with Norway, and the Komi and the Nentsi of the northwest. The Chukchi and Koryak peoples of the northeast follow a similar way of life to the Eskimos or Inuit of Canada.

A hunter skis cross-country

Travelling east

Eastern Siberia is another bitterly cold region. In the city of Yakutsk the schools only close when the temperature drops to minus 50°C (minus 58°F)! When this happens, lessons continue on television.

Towns may be 800 kilometres (500 miles) apart. Yakutia, the homeland of the Yakut people, is about the size of India. However its population is only a million.

Beyond Siberia is the Russian Federation's Far East. The native people are now greatly outnumbered by Russians, who have settled here since the

In Yakutsk, milk is sold in frozen blocks!

These Koreans live on the Russian island of Sakhalin.

1880s. The Russian Far East is rich in natural resources. It has forests, rich fishing grounds, and oil, coal and other minerals underground.

Chains of high mountains rise beyond the Lena River. To the north, the Verkhoyansk, Chersky and Kolyma ranges stretch towards the Chukchi Peninsula. To the south are the Yablonovy and Stanovoy ranges. The River Amur marks the border between the Russian Federation and China. A volcano on the Kamchatka peninsula, Mt Klyuchevskaya, is the highest mountain in the region, at a height of 4750 metres (15 580 ft). There are thirty active volcanoes on Kamchatka and on the island of Sakhalin, across the Sea of Okhotsk.

There are plans to bring prosperity to the whole region between the city of Vladivostok and the Tumen Delta, in China. In the next 20 years a new city may be built, with a harbour and canal, linked to a new road, rail and air network. The cost of this development will be around $30 billion. The plan is backed by the United Nations and other international organizations.

Pacific Russia

From the Russian island of Ratmanov there is a view across the Bering Strait to the mountains of Alaska, one of the United States. The Russians once owned this territory, but sold it to the Americans in 1867.

Over the last hundred years Russia has quarrelled over its eastern borders many times. There have been serious disputes with both China and Japan. Today there is still disagreement over who owns some of the Kurile Islands, to the north of Japan.

Vladivostok

The biggest city on Russia's Pacific coast is the port of Vladivostok, on the Sea of Japan. It is 9288 kilometres (5771 miles) from Moscow. In fact it is nearer to San Francisco, in the United States, than it is to the Russian capital! The population is around 600 000. Vladivostok is an important naval base. Ferries to Japan leave from the smaller port of Nakhodka, 88 kilometres (55 miles) to the east.

The port of Vladivostok at night

Moscow

The vast area of the Russian Federation, from the Baltic Sea to the Pacific Ocean, is governed from Moscow. Today this is a large city of about 9 million people, on the Moscow River in the heart of European Russia. Once it was just a wooden fort on a hill. We know that Moscow existed in the year 1147, when a prince called Yuri Dolgoruky ('long arm') gave a banquet there.

A map of modern Moscow shows that it is surrounded by 'rings'. The outermost is the 'Golden Ring', a chain of ancient monasteries which guarded the approaches to the city long ago. The monasteries are set amongst woods of silver birch. Then comes the Moscow motorway ring and the steel ring of the circle railway. Next comes the 'Garden Ring'. This is no longer as green as it sounds, for it was made into a wide road in 1935. The 'Boulevard Ring' however has pleasant tree-lined paths down the central reservation of the ring road. The paths make up a walk of about eight kilometres (five miles) around the inner city. Then, right at the centre, is a final 'ring' – formed by the walls of the Kremlin.

Kremlin is a Russian word for 'fort'. There are *kremlins* in many Russian cities. Moscow's present Kremlin dates back 500 years. Its tall red walls stretch for 2230 metres (nearly 1.5 miles) around Borovitsky Hill. Inside there are palaces, golden-domed cathedrals, offices, museums and parks and a 400 year-old cannon. The Kremlin was the centre of Soviet political power but the Russian Parliament now meets in the White House, a modern building near the river.

The walls and towers of the Kremlin, on the banks of the Moscow River

The Kremlin walls contain the tombs of many famous Russians, including heroes of the communist period.

The city spreads out from the Kremlin on both sides of the Moscow River and beyond. There are famous parks and statues, huge government buildings from the 1930s, department stores and modern hotels. Fashionable shopping streets such as Arbat contrast with factories and suburban blocks of flats.

A centre of communications

Moscow's Metro is spectacular. This underground railway was opened in 1935 and many of its stations have chandeliers, marble columns and statues. Its trains carry five million passengers a day!

Moscow is at the centre of a national and international rail and air network. Although Moscow is far from the sea, its river and canals link up with the White, Black, Baltic, Caspian and Azov Seas. Barges are used to transport grain, timber and industrial goods.

St Basil's Cathedral towers over Moscow's Red Square.

Smiling through the Moscow winter

Out and about

Red Square This huge open space is next to the Kremlin. The name comes from the Russian word for 'beautiful' (once the same word in Russian as 'red'). It is the site of many big parades and political demonstrations.

The coloured domes and towers of **St Basil's Cathedral** were completed in 1560. The cathedral was built in memory of the Russian victory over the Tartars.

GUM was built 100 years ago as a smart shopping arcade. The name stands for State Universal Store. Many people now buy from street stalls but 350 000 shoppers visit the new shops and cafés in GUM each day.

Russia at work

Many Russians led a wretched life in the nineteenth century – they were little better than slaves. When the communists or Bolsheviks came to power in 1917 they aimed to change all that. Power was to be given to the ordinary working people.

The Red Flag of the Soviet Union included the emblem of a hammer and sickle, to show the power of factory and farm workers. The communists put up huge statues of heroic men and women at work. Russia was modernised. New factories were built. The economy was planned and directed by the government.

Many of these changes were successful, but others brought social unrest, causing hardship and hunger. The government became controlled by ruthless leaders who took on more and more powers. Some people were forced to work on government projects as prisoners.

By the 1970s life in the Soviet Union had become easier but sometimes state-owned factories were not run efficiently or fairly. There were many shortages.

After 1991 the new Russian government tried to move towards a 'free market', like the capitalist countries of Western Europe and the Americas. Some factories and farms were put up for private sale. Foreign businesses moved into Russia and advertising hoardings appeared on the streets.

Today Russia is going through great changes. A few businessmen have become rich quickly, but for most people

A statue of a factory worker and a farmer dates from the communist period.

Herding cattle in Karelia

there are still many shortages and queues in the shops. There are new problems as well, such as high unemployment. Many Russians still support the communist approach to economics, but others believe that the recent changes will one day lead to prosperity.

Natural wealth

The Russian Federation ought to be wealthy. It has some of the world's richest reserves of minerals. There are huge fields of coal, oil and natural gas. The Ural Mountains contain iron ore, copper, gold and precious stones. Central Siberia may have once been a remote wilderness, but today it is the power house of industry, despite its distance from Moscow.

Russia has vast forests and fishing grounds. Cattle are raised in European Russia and southwest Siberia. The southern steppes produce wheat, barley and maize.

Russia's enormous size has its disadvantages. Transporting goods over such long distances is very expensive.

Power and pollution

The Soviet Union made little attempt to control the harmful waste from factories. Over the years this waste has destroyed people's health as well as the landscape. In the Russian Federation, nuclear power stations still have a poor safety record. Since 1992 there have been 205 dangerous incidents, including a major disaster at Tomsk. Even so, today's government wants to double its output of nuclear power.

Space research

The Soviet Union built special cities for its researchers and scientists.

It became a world leader in space technology and sent the first man and woman into space. In 1993 the Russians used a space mirror to reflect sunlight on to the Earth. One day this project might spell the end of long Siberian winters.

Timber and factory chimneys, Novosibirsk

Living from day to day

Even the tobacconist's shop has a long queue outside.

During the period of communist rule, prices did not rise for 70 years. These days, some prices are no longer controlled. Many shopkeepers can charge what they like. Rents and fares have risen. The rouble, the Russian unit of money, is worth less compared with foreign currencies such as the US dollar or the German mark.

The Communist Party used to have great control over peoples' lives. Many people obeyed the rules and regulations in the Soviet Union out of fear.

However the communist government did provide security. It guaranteed child care, health care, free education, a job and housing. Providing all these benefits meant that the Soviet Union had to borrow large sums of money from other governments.

In 1992 the new President of the Russian Federation, Boris Yeltsin, warned the Russian people that 'things must get worse before they get better'. Russians have many new freedoms, but many new problems.

Traditional Russian buildings are of carved wood.

Housing and homes

Most city-dwellers in Russia live in small, crowded flats. Some people get together as a group to buy or build a block of flats. Each family then pays back a share of the cost. This arrangement is called a housing co-operative.

In the countryside, more people live in small houses. Many of these are traditional wooden houses, which look pretty but often have no piped water or electricity. Many Russian homes were destroyed during the Second World War. During the 1950s the government built cheap blocks of flats as quickly as they could. Many families lived in communal flats. In these, each family has one room and shares a kitchen and bathroom with other families. Even now, half of all Russian couples live with their parents. The communist government had planned to house every family in a separate home by the year 2000.

However, the changes in government have brought their own problems. Many Russians are returning home from parts of the old Soviet Union that are now independent states. They have nowhere to live.

Until 1991 many Russian soldiers were stationed in central Europe, in countries such as East Germany and Poland. Most of these soldiers have now returned, adding to the number of homeless people. The families of 200 000 soldiers are now living in tents in the Russian Federation.

Sharing a kitchen, in St Petersburg

Food and drink

Each region has special dishes but some traditional Russian food is eaten throughout the Russian Federation. *Borshch* is a soup made from beetroots cooked in stock, and served either hot or chilled. *Beef stroganov* is thin strips of fillet steak cooked with mushrooms, onions, black pepper and soured cream. Little pancakes called *blinis* are made from buckwheat flour.

Russia's many rivers and lakes provide a wealth of freshwater fish, for which there are many recipes. The greatest delicacy of all is fish roe, or caviar – Russians love it. The biggest and most expensive of these roe, or eggs, are the 'black pearls' produced by the Beluga sturgeon. This fish lives in the Caspian Sea and grows to a length of four metres (14 ft). Red caviar is salmon roe.

Melons, fruit and salads for a feast

Tea is served from a samovar.

Tea from the *samovar*

Samovars have been used to heat tea in
Russia for about 700 years. Traditional
samovars are heated by burning charcoal,
but modern ones use electricity. A
samovar is a large urn in which water is
boiled and then poured through a tap into
a pot of strong tea. A china teapot is kept
warm by being placed on top of the
samovar. It may be covered with a cosy in
the form of a special doll which has thick,
padded skirts.

Russians drink tea without adding milk.
They may sweeten their tea with jam, or
put a hard sugar lump in their mouth and
sip the tea through the sugar.

Russians like to drink vodka, a very
strong, clear alcoholic spirit. Vodka was
originally made from wheat, but now
other grains or potatoes may be used.
Russians also drink beer, sparkling wines
or *kvas* – a weak drink made from bread
and honey. *Kvas* is sold on street corners
by old ladies.

Eating in or out

For years luxury foods have been too
expensive to buy and Russian shops often
have empty shelves. However people do
like to sit around the table eating,
drinking, talking or celebrating a family
birthday. They will always find something
to offer a guest.

In recent years new cafés, food stalls
and kiosks have began to appear along
the streets and in parks. They sell coffee
or hot meat snacks such as *shashlik* or
kebab. Foreign companies such as
McDonalds and Pizza Hut have brought
the idea of 'fast food' into Russia, but
their restaurants are very expensive by
Russian standards.

Shopping for food in a Moscow store

Leisure and the arts

Champion gymnast Sergei Charkov, 1993

Russians are great lovers of sport and have broken many Olympic and world records. Skating and gymnastics are popular sports. Football clubs such as Moscow Dynamo have a large following in the summer. In winter, people go to see ice hockey matches, and they like to watch all kinds of sport on television.

Because homes are often small and crowded, Russians go out a lot. They play chess in the open air, even in winter, and parks have summer boating lakes and winter ice rinks. People meet friends at public baths, relaxing in the steam room or taking a cold plunge.

There are seven public holidays each year, and most workers also have annual holidays of three or four weeks. Schools close for three months in the summer. Many children go to summer camps or family holidays at the sea or in the mountains. They may spend all summer with their grandparents at the family's holiday home, or *dacha*, in the countryside.

Many city dwellers go to a *dacha* at weekends. It may be as small as a wooden shed, but there is normally a

Picture frames by Fabergé, jeweller to the tsars

small garden for growing fruit and vegetables and a river nearby for fishing.

At New Year, Grandfather Frost brings presents to children in a sleigh.

The Russian Orthodox Christians celebrate Christmas Day on 7 January, because they follow a different calendar. Christmas was not an official holiday during the years of communist rule.

Icons and paintings

Some of the oldest Russian paintings are called icons. The painting of an icon is a religious act. The painter must pray and fast before beginning to paint. Candle-lit icons were once placed in every home and out of doors at crossroads, as well as in churches and cathedrals.

During the 1880s and 1890s many Russian painters followed a realistic style. Experimental art and design were popular until the end of the 1920s, but in the 1930s and 40s painters were expected to show heroic views of workers in a very realistic style. Today artists are free to produce and sell work in any style.

The world of books

Russians are great readers. You see people reading on buses and metro trains, in parks and in cafes. Russia has produced many of the world's greatest poets, novelists and playwrights. These include Alexander Pushkin (1799-1837), Leo Tolstoy (1828-1910) and Anton Chekhov (1860-1904).

In the spotlight

Tickets for puppet shows, cinemas, circuses, theatres, ballet, opera and concerts all sell out quickly.

A hundred years ago St Petersburg was a great centre of ballet. Today people come to Russia from all over the world to see performances by the dancers of the Kirov ballet and the Bolshoi, in Moscow. The music for some of the most famous ballets are by the composer Peter Tchaikovsky (1840-93).

Many of Russia's greatest composers were inspired by folk music. Some folk musicians play a three-sided string instrument called a *balalaika*.

The Kirov Ballet from St Petersburg performs Tchaikovsky's Swan Lake.

Russia's beginnings

St Sergius founded the monastery at Sergiev in 1337.

The Russians have been called the 'people of the plains'. Between Poland and Central Siberia there are few mountains. For thousands of years warriors and herders moved across the open grassy steppes of the south or explored the great rivers, through the northern forests. Russia became a battleground between the peoples of Europe and Asia, but it was also a meeting place for different ways of life and cultures.

The first people to live in the land that now makes up the Russian Federation were Stone Age hunters who moved from Asia towards the Baltic Sea. About 2500 years ago the southern steppes were the home of Scythians, fierce horsemen who were famous for their archery. While Asian nomads controlled the southern steppes, eastern Slavs from Europe were soon pushing into western and northern forests. During the ninth century AD, Viking warriors and traders from Scandinavia rowed down the rivers of eastern Europe, attacking villages and taking slaves.

The country around the rivers Dvina, Dniepr and Volga became known as Rus, and the first Russian state grew up here, with Kiev as its capital. Kiev, Novgorod and Smolensk became great trading centres, selling fur from beyond the Urals into Europe. Christianity came to the region over 1000 years ago, from the Byzantine Empire, far to the south in what is now Greece and Turkey.

Russia had long been threatened by the Tartars, a Mongol people from the far east. After the 1220s the Tartars attacked and invaded large areas of European Russia. Germans and Swedes attacked Russia from the west. Prince Alexander Nevsky of Novgorod became a hero by defeating both in the 1240s.

A film made by Sergei Eisenstein in 1938 told the story of Alexander Nevsky.

The first *tsars*

Moscow was becoming more powerful. Grand Prince Ivan III (Ivan 'the Great' who reigned 1462-1505) was the first Russian leader to call himself *tsar*, or emperor. He married a niece of the Byzantine emperor and took the two-headed eagle of Byzantium as the symbol of Russia.

His grandson, Ivan IV (1530-84) was only three years old when he came to the throne in 1533. He ruled over new lands to the east, in Siberia, and subdued the Tartars. He became known as Ivan 'the Terrible' because he was a violent and cruel man.

Ivan's son Fedor was too weak to rule and had no heir. A noble called Boris Godunov seized the throne in 1598. When he died in 1605 there was a 'time of troubles'. Sweden invaded the north and Poles occupied Moscow. A revolt by peasants was savagely put down.

A great empire

Peter the Great studies shipbuilding in England.

Tsar Peter I ('the Great', reigned 1682-1725) was determined to bring changes to his country. He went to Holland and England in secret and worked in the shipyards, learning how to build a navy. His armies won battles against Sweden, Turkey and Persia. He won control of land on the Baltic coast and built the great port of St Petersburg as Russia's 'window on the west'. He even made his nobles cut off their long beards, which he thought were old-fashioned!

In 1762 Tsar Peter III was murdered and his wife, Catherine the Great

The royal sleigh of Catherine the Great

(reigned 1762-96) became Empress of Russia. Under her rule Russia's borders extended, to take in Poles, Ukrainians, Lithuanians and Belarussians. Russia now ruled the Black Sea coast and the steppes of the southeast. In 1773 there was a great revolt around the Volga and the Urals. The revolt was led by Emelian Pugachev, a Cossack who claimed to have been the *tsar*. In 1775 Pugachev was betrayed, taken to Moscow in an iron cage and executed.

The empire at war

In 1812 the French emperor Napoleon led an army of 675 000 men into Russia. Like other invaders before him Napoleon had not realised how harsh a Russian winter could be. Nine out of every ten French soldiers died in the snow, during a disastrous retreat from Moscow. Further wars were fought against France and Britain in the Crimea (1854-56) and against Japan (1904-05).

Foreign wars were expensive, and hungry workers and peasants had to pay high taxes. Returning soldiers brought home new political ideas and many Russians began to demand a just society, fair wages and a democratic vote.

Until 1861, when Tsar Alexander II (reigned 1855-81) brought in new laws, many Russian peasants were serfs, who were forced to work on the estates where they were born. Even after these changes many people lived in misery. More and more people began to join secret organisations which wanted to change society and fight injustice. One of these groups, called the 'People's Will', killed Alexander II with a bomb.

In 1905 a great revolution broke out in St Petersburg. Tsar Nicholas II (reigned 1894-1917) was forced to give in and create a parliament, but it had little power. When Russia went to war against Germany in 1914 it seemed that a new revolution might break out at any time. It took just three years.

Hungry families queue for soup in tsarist St Petersburg

Red, white and blue

During the First World War Russian armies fought against Germany and Austria. By 1917 the soldiers had little food and few weapons. There were strikes and demonstrations on the streets in Russia. Soldiers were refusing to obey orders.

In March 1917 the parliament took power from the Tsar, but the war with Germany continued. V.I.Lenin, the revolutionary who had been in exile in Switzerland, returned to Russia through German territory. That November he and his supporters known as 'Bolsheviks', seized power. This event is known as the

Revolutionary 'Red Guards' light a fire on the streets of Petrograd in October 1917.

October Revolution, because of its date in the old Russian calendar. The red flag of revolution now flew in the streets.

Many Russians fled the country. The 'Reds' were fought by the anti-revolutionaries, or 'Whites'. Foreign powers sent arms and troops to the Whites, but by 1922 these were defeated by the Red Army, which was led by Leon Trotsky (1879-1940). The new communist republics joined together to form the Union of Soviet Socialist Republics (USSR or Soviet Union).

A brief friendship – Soviet and American troops meet up on the River Elbe in 1945.

Lenin died in 1924. During his illness he had been followed as leader by a Georgian called Joseph Dzhugashvili, who as a young man had taken the name of Stalin ('man of steel'). Stalin's drive to create a new industrial nation was achieved through terror. Peasants starved to death because of his policies, and even old communist revolutionaries were imprisoned and executed. As in the days of the *tsars*, the secret police were feared.

A Second World War

After a brief alliance with Germany, the Soviet Union joined sides with Britain and United States in the Second World War. No other nation was to suffer such severe losses – at least 20 million Russians died. The Germans invaded the Soviet Union, but the courageous defence of the city of Stalingrad (Volgograd) in 1942-43 marked a turning point. In 1945 the Red Army invaded Germany and met up with American troops along the River Elbe.

Cold War to *glasnost*

The Soviet Union now controlled countries right across Central Europe. This 'bloc' was opposed by the capitalist countries, such as the United States. Both sides now owned powerful nuclear weapons but this 'Cold War' of mistrust did not turn into another world war. Three years after Stalin's death, Nikita Krushchev dared to criticise the period of rule by Stalin. People thought things had changed but Krushchev was replaced as leader in 1964.

Reforms did not begin until 1985, when Mikhail Gorbachev became leader of the Communist Party. He signed the first treaty between the Soviet Union and the United States to reduce the number of nuclear weapons. His main ideas were *perestroika*, which means 'reconstruction', or rebuilding something in a different way, and *glasnost*, which means 'openness'.

Gorbachev was more popular abroad than he was at home. In 1991 Boris Yeltsin was elected President of Russia and the communist Soviet Union came to an end. On New Year's Day 1992 the red, white and blue flag of the Russian Federation replaced the Soviet flag flying over the Kremlin.

These traditional Russian dolls have been made to look like Russia's political leaders.

Fact file

Flags and emblems

The flag of the Russian Federation is a tricolour of red, white and blue. This flag was first used by Peter the Great in 1694. National emblems include the double-headed eagle of Byzantium and the hammer-and-sickle of the communist period.

National anthem

In March 1993 Boris Yeltsin announced that a competition would be held for words to a new national anthem for the Russian Federation. The music is a hundred years old.

Government

In December 1993 the Russian people voted for President Yeltsin's new constitution, giving the president more powers to govern the country. The new Federal Assembly has two houses. The Federal Council, or upper house, has 178 seats. The State Duma, or lower house, has 450 seats. Half of the candidates for the Duma are elected from constituencies. The rest are elected from lists of candidates drawn up by the political parties.

Religion

Under communist rule, religious worship was discouraged. People are now free to follow their own beliefs. Many people are still atheists who do not believe in God. Most Christians follow the Russian Orthodox Church, but there are also Protestants and Roman Catholics. Buddhist temples and Islamic mosques are opening again.

Money

The unit of currency is the rouble. The old banknotes for 3, 25 and 50 roubles showed a picture of Lenin. The new 100 and 500 rouble notes show the Russian flag flying from the Kremlin instead. New coins are replacing notes up to 100 roubles.

Education

Children must go to school for 10 years from the ages of 6 to 16. Education is free. University students receive a grant.

Newspapers and television

Most of today's newspapers were started during the period of communist rule. *Pravda*, founded by Lenin in 1912, was the newspaper of the Communist Party. The biggest selling papers are now *Trud* and *Komsomolskaya Pravda*. *Today* was started in 1993 and is the first private Russian newspaper financed by advertisements.

There are six television channels. Only one channel broadcasts to the whole area of the old Soviet Union. Russian TV broadcasts throughout the Russian Federation. Channel 6 is foreign-owned and shows American films and news as well as Russian programmes.

Some famous people

Alexander Nevsky (1220-63) defeated Swedish and German invasions

Andrei Rublyev (c1360-1430), Russia's most important religious painter

Catherine the Great (1729-96) was German but ruled Russia for over 34 years

Leo Tolstoy (1828-1910) was a political thinker and great writer

Ivan Pavlov (1849-1936) studied the workings of the brain and won the Nobel Prize for medicine

Vladimir Ilyich Lenin (1870-1924), communist revolutionary.

Grigory Rasputin (1871-1916), a monk who was believed to have mystical powers by the wife of the last *tsar*

Anna Pavlova (1885-1931) trained as a ballerina in St Petersburg and founded her own ballet company

Sergei Eisenstein (1898-1948) directed many films about Russian history

Sergci Korolev (1906-66) designed the world's first spacecraft

Dmitri Shostakovich (1906-75) wrote music in many forms

Alexander Solzhenitsyn (1918-) wrote about the horrors of prison camps set up by Stalin

Andrei Sakharov (1921-89) was a physicist and politician

Mastislav Rostropovich (1927-) is a cellist and conductor

Yuri Gagarin (1934-1968) was the first man in space

Valentina Tereshkova (1937-) was the first woman in space

Olga Korbut (1955 -) won three Olympic medals for gymnastics in 1972

Some key events in history

c440 BC Attila the Hun led attacks from the east

AD **862** Rurik, a Varangian prince, became the first leader of the Slavs

988 Grand Duke Vladimir of Kiev became a Christian

1237-38 the Tartar invasion and fall of Kiev

1480 Ivan III won battles against the Tartars. Russian cities came under control of Moscow

1547 Ivan IV introduced serfdom

1613 Michael became first *tsar* of the Romanov family

1713 St Petersburg became new capital of Russia

1783 Catherine the Great won control of the Crimea, the last Tartar stronghold

1812 Napoleon retreated from Moscow

1861 Abolition of serfdom

1905 Revolution forced the *tsar* to hold elections

1917 Bolsheviks seized power

1918 The last Romanov *tsar*, Nicholas II, was shot with his family

1942-43 the city of Stalingrad was successfully defended against the German army

1953 Death of Joseph Stalin

1979 Soviet Union invaded Afghanistan

1985 Mikhail Gorbachev became leader of the Communist Party

1990 Communists voted to end one-party rule

1991 Gorbachev resigned

1992 Russian flag flew over the Kremlin in Moscow

Index